Giving Together

an adventure in generosity

Author of Gospel Patrons
JOHN RINEHART

For Jesus,
who wrote my name in heaven!

The Map

Base Camp 9

Generous people make an enormous difference in the world and have a lot of fun doing it. Now is the time to go on a journey to become those kinds of people.

☐ Assemble Your Team

Invest in Identity 23

God offers us the antidote to anxiety about money. It takes tenacity to believe him and step forward, but this is the way forward.

☐ 5-Day Foundation

Start Small 39

God wants to free us from the trap of thinking more money will make us happy. The world has it upside down. The real connection between money and happiness is not what we've been told.

☐ We Are The Church Experiment

Commit to Community 57

God is molding his followers into an elite team. We can push against this and remain a collection of individuals, or we can opt in and do something great. The choice is ours.

☐ 90-Day Giving Challenge

Redefine Rewards 71

God wired us to chase rewards, but which rewards will you chase? Now is the time to decide because what you do with your life will echo into eternity.

☐ Rich Young Ruler Experience

Practice Partnership 89

God has an amazing part you can play in his kingdom. You don't have to be somebody else or do what they do. You just have to be willing to partner with others.

☐ Ask It Exercise

Intend Impact 103

God is looking for people to use. He offers us the chance to stop watching the news and go out and make it instead. The first step is just outside your comfort zone.

☐ The Greatest Time To Be Alive

Summiting 127

God is guiding you to the peak. Summiting is never easy, but you have come a long way in this adventure and you will surely make it to the end.

The Plan

You have an exciting adventure ahead. Here's what to expect:

Together

This book is called *Giving Together* because it's designed for you to go through it *together* with others. You could invite your family, a few friends, your small group from church, a book club, a prayer group or a few colleagues from work. It's meant to be an adventure you go on together.

Reading

You have seven chapters to read, plus a short conclusion. Each chapter can be read in 15-20 minutes. Several teams have found it best to have someone read the chapters aloud at each of their meetings instead of asking everyone to read on their own. This also ensures the content is fresh in everyone's minds.

Training Exercises

This will be more than a discussion group. You will have seven training exercises to complete. You'll begin each exercise as a group and then there will be a piece to complete individually before you meet again. When you gather back together it's important to make the time to share your experiences with one another.

Videos

Along with each training exercise, I'll share a short video that the team leader might like to forward to everyone for extra encouragement. It will look like this:

THIS WEEK'S VIDEO:
givingtogether.video/basecamp

I trust that in every step you take on this adventure, God is going to meet you with fresh encouragement, insight, and joy.

Let's go further up and further in,

John

Base Camp

I once had the chance to jump out of an airplane, but the truth is I didn't jump. No, my jumpsuit was tightly attached to a guy I had known for less than an hour. I had no choice but to believe him when he said he had done this a few hundred times.

When our plane got up to 12,000 feet and the glass door opened, we scooted over toward the wind. My jumpmaster sat on the edge of the plane while I dangled in front of him outside. Then he yelled, "1 ... 2 ... 3" and flung us out into the wide-open sky.

Free
    f
      a
        l
          l

It wasn't rational. Skydiving doesn't make sense. And as every first-timer knows, when the door on the plane opens, everything within you says, "This is crazy!"

Giving is a lot like skydiving. Sometimes you have to be flung out of the plane to get started – but once you've done it, it's exhilarating.

If this is your first jump into giving, "Hi, my name is John. I've done this a few hundred times. I'll be your jumpmaster."

Floor It

Giving is the opposite of what you've heard. It's not a duty; it's an adventure. It's not an obligation; it's a joy. Giving will cause your world to grow bigger and your heart to grow happier.

I believe God made you to be a giver. The enemy wants to slow you down. I want to help you floor it.

The premise of this book is that God wants to use you. He has a part for you to play and generosity is your on-ramp to playing it.

I've been on my own journey of generosity for years. My first book, *Gospel Patrons*, was about how God uses generous people to change the world. This book is about how we become those kinds of people. *Gospel Patrons* was a book of vision. This is a book about action. You have the chance to make a difference in this world and I don't want you to miss it.

Ten Convictions

Base camp is the place to prepare before you get to elevation. It's where you talk as a team before you ascend. There are certain things you'll need to know to be ready for the adventure ahead. So as we get started, here are the ten convictions driving this book.

1. God is the greatest giver. The repeated chorus of Scripture is that the God of the Bible is rich and generous.[1] God doesn't need our money. So this book will not guilt you to give more. Instead, it's an invitation to learn to be generous and bear the family resemblance of our Father in heaven.

2. Giving is about our hearts. Jesus talked more about money and possessions than anything else. He understood the pressures and anxieties we all face.[2] He also knew the pull of the world to make money our ultimate goal.[3] And he wants more for us than that. Jesus wants to train each of us to use the money he's given us in a way

---

1   2 Samuel 12:7–8; Psalm 24:1; Psalm 50:10–11; Matthew 7:11; John 3:16; Romans 5:8; Galatians 2:20
2   Matthew 6:25–34
3   Matthew 6:24; Mark 4:19; Mark 8:36

that honors him, loves people, and sets our hearts free. Giving is about more than money; it's about our hearts.[4]

3. Giving increases our joy. Generous people are happy people. Jesus promised it and studies of all different kinds have proven this.[5] As you take your first steps on this adventure, I trust you will experience more joy too.

4. Giving draws us closer to God. We see in Scripture that God has a heartbeat of generosity. The more we learn to give like him, the closer we come to God's heart. Giving melts away our focus on ourselves and we begin to live as we were made to live, for the glory of God and the good of others.

5. Giving connects us to our purpose. History is not just made by preachers and missionaries. God has used generous people from all kinds of professions to advance his kingdom – and he's not done yet. Giving is a way to get in the game and join God's work in the world.

6. We need a fresh start with money. You and I have heard thousands of sermons on money. TV, movies, magazines, ads, books, friends and parents have all been preaching about it. Our views of money have been shaped more by the world than by the word of

---

4   Matthew 6:21
5   Acts 20:35

God. We need a reset in our relationship with money – a reset with God as our foundation.

7. We need to talk honestly about money. Money is something we think about all the time, but rarely talk about, even with the people closest to us. But the first step to any change is to start talking. If you want to get in shape, you join a gym or hire a personal trainer and start talking about your fitness goals. If you want to improve your marriage you'll attend a weekend seminar or meet with a marriage therapist so you can talk honestly about how to grow. If you want to stop drinking too much, you go to Alcoholics Anonymous meetings and start talking with others. This is how growth works, so if we want to be people who grow in generosity, we have to start talking about money and giving.

8. Now is the time to learn about giving. We can keep telling ourselves we'll give later, but there will always be a later. Now is the time to learn to be faithful with what we have. Generosity is not something for other people richer than us. We all have the opportunity to be givers, whether we have a lot or a little, because generosity is not an amount; it's a mindset. Now is the time to adopt a generous mindset.

9. We learn to give by giving. It's not enough to read a book about exercise or watch exercise videos. At some point you have to put the book down and do something. The same is true in giving. The real learning happens in the doing. So after reading and talking about generosity, I want you to practice it. At the end of every chapter there will be one simple way you can apply it. Think of it like going to the gym. I want to help you get in giving shape.

10. We need a team around us. Matt Walker, an international mountain guide, has said, "Without great companionship we may have amazing experiences, but we don't walk away with an adventure."[6] I want you to have a life-changing adventure and that begins by inviting others to join you. You could start with your family, a few friends, your small group from church, a book club, a prayer group or a few colleagues from work. Tell them this will be more than a discussion group. It's meant to be an adventure you go on together.

The Adventure Together

Before these pages were ever published I led a group of men through each chapter and each exercise. I wanted to see if it worked. So we met weekly: an insurance salesman, an artist, a crane mechanic, a business owner, a film producer, and me. I read them each chapter out loud, we discussed it, and then left to go and put it into practice that week.

---

6   *The Five Elements of Adventure*, dir. by Diana Ellis Hill (2015; Xtreme Videos, 2018 video).

What we found was that our joy went way up and our worry went way down. God used us to impact people who we otherwise wouldn't have, and we were changed by God in the process.

So I tried this experience a second time with a group of young professionals in Silicon Valley. Their stories of faith and generosity were so inspiring that one guy said, "*Giving Together* was like the training wheels that taught me a new way to live."

I want this for you – a new freedom, a new joy and a new adventure. So if you're ready, then scoot to the open door with me.

1 ... 2 ... 3 ... Here we go!

Assemble
Your Team

TRAINING EXERCISE 1

Assemble
Your Team

Step 1   Your first step is to assemble your team. Who would you like to join you on this journey? Pray and then write down five or six names that come to mind:

Name 1   _____

Name 2   _____

Name 3   _____

Name 4   _____

Name 5   _____

Name 6   _____

Step 2   Invite your team together. You may want to reread Base Camp aloud to them to cast the vision for this experience. Next you'll need to decide where and when you'll meet. It could be once a week, once a month, or once a quarter. Decide what's going to work for you and your team and then schedule your next six meetings:

Date 1 _____

Date 2 _____

Date 3 _____

Date 4 _____

Date 5 _____

Date 6 _____

Step 3   Before you leave base camp, you'll want your team to know each other. So ask each person to share:

"How would you describe your upbringing with money? And what feelings did you associate with it?"

Step 4   Then, ask each person:

"Look back at the ten convictions. Which one most stood out to you and why?"

Step 5   Take a few minutes to write down your hopes and expectations for the adventure ahead. Share these with one another.

_____

_____

_____

_____

_____

_____

_____

Step 6   Pray together, committing this adventure to the Lord. Invite God to work in you and through you. Ask him to lead you every step of the way.

THIS WEEK'S VIDEO:

givingtogether.video/basecamp

Invest in Identity

For most of my life I lived as if God and money were two separate subjects that barely, if ever, overlapped. I grew up in a hard-working middle class family. Both of my parents were one generation removed from farming so they valued hard work and certainly taught it to their two boys. I delivered newspapers at age 11 and from the time I was 16 I was almost always working. Retail, restaurants, landscaping, odd jobs – anything that would help me pay for college. I came to view money as the exchange for hard work.

I don't remember our family ever praying about money. Perhaps my parents did behind closed doors, but to me money seemed like the kind of thing that you don't pray about. Money was our responsibility and God had very little to do with it.

But from a young age I found that this approach wasn't working.

Money = Stress

As a ten-year-old I asked my parents how much money they had in the bank. I don't know why I asked. I don't know why it mattered. But they told me and I remember feeling stressed – like there wasn't enough.

When I was 12 all the cool kids in my school wore the cool jeans. So I asked for a pair for Christmas and lo and behold, Mom and Dad (or Santa Claus) actually bought them for me. I felt awesome for about five minutes, until the thought of how much money was spent on a pair of jeans made me ask to return them.

Money equaled stress. I felt it from a young age and it continued into my twenties.

When my wife and I got married, we were deep in student loan debt and I may have been the cheapest husband on the planet. I remember one time Renée called me from the store to ask if she could spend three dollars on sponges to clean the kitchen sink. I said, "No, we don't have three dollars. That money belongs to someone else."

I'm guessing you have your own stories. They may not be about jeans and sponges, but most of us have experienced anxiety surrounding money. We know wealth is uncertain.[1] It might be here today, but it could easily be gone tomorrow. Markets crash. Tax laws change. Medical emergencies happen. Moth and rust destroy and thieves break in and steal.[2]

---

1   1 Timothy 6:17
2   Matthew 6:19

So our instinct is to worry, to hustle, to squirrel away enough money to conquer the fear. But it doesn't work. More money does not solve the fear we feel inside. Rich and poor alike worry about money. Some of us worry about keeping it and others about getting it. Some of us seek after it for security and others for survival. The more we try to hang on to our money, the more we fear the day when it will sprout wings and fly away.[3]

So what are we to do?

I'm here to say that as I have followed Jesus, I have seen a different way, a better path, that I aspire to walk down. I hope you'll come with me.

The Path of Peace

The path Jesus lays out for us is the path of peace. At the center of his most famous sermon (known as 'the Sermon on the Mount'), Jesus says, "Do not be anxious about your life, what you will eat or what you will drink, nor about your body, what you will put on."[4]

But the question becomes, "How?" How do we stop being anxious about money? How can we keep money from dominating our thoughts and controlling our decisions?

Jesus doesn't recommend a budgeting seminar. His advice is not to build up passive income or retirement savings so that you

---

3   Proverbs 23:4–5
4   Matthew 6:25

have enough money laid up for many years.[5] Instead, Jesus' shocking counsel is to look at birds and flowers. None of us saw that coming. But that's what Jesus says. Listen:

> *"Look at the birds of the air: they neither sow nor reap nor gather into barns, and yet your heavenly Father feeds them. Are you not of more value than they? And which of you by being anxious can add a single hour to his span of life? And why are you anxious about clothing? Consider the lilies of the field, how they grow: they neither toil nor spin, yet I tell you, even Solomon in all his glory was not arrayed like one of these. But if God so clothes the grass of the field, which today is alive and tomorrow is thrown into the oven, will he not much more clothe you, O you of little faith? Therefore do not be anxious, saying, 'What shall we eat?' or 'What shall we drink?' or 'What shall we wear?' For the Gentiles seek after all these things, and your heavenly Father knows that you need them all. But seek first the kingdom of God and his righteousness, and all these things will be added to you."[6]*

Despite how many times you may have read or heard this passage, this is no simplistic, sentimental, hippy answer: "Just look at flowers and all your money problems will go away." As 21st-century

---

5   This was the strategy of the rich man who Jesus called a fool in Luke 12:13–21.
6   Matthew 6:26–33

people it can be tempting to think this is a primitive first-century approach that we have advanced beyond. But we must remember, Jesus was speaking words that would never pass away.[7] His answer is not shallow, but instead a word for every generation, every culture, every people. Jesus is speaking to the first and third world, the rich and poor, the literate and illiterate. This is truth on fire!

Jesus' remedy for anxiety is a call to look at the birds of the air and the flowers of field, and then to look beyond them. He wants you to see that the God who holds out his hand each morning to the birds, making sure each one gets enough food, is your heavenly Father. The one who dresses each lily of the field in royal robes is not just the King of creation; he's also your Father. You mean more to him than birds and flowers. You are his child.

The path of peace begins with the hard work of believing that you are the son or daughter of a great King and a good Father.

Rising Higher

Several years ago, my wife and I had the chance to hike in the Himalayan Mountains. We flew from Kathmandu into this tiny town called Lukla where we began our trek at an elevation of 9,400 feet. We walked up and down the narrow trails, crossing rivers on hanging bridges, traversing paths with Sherpas and yaks. Our guide jokingly called us "the slug team" because we were apparently that

---

7   Matthew 24:35

slow. We went as far as a village called Tengboche, reaching almost 13,000 feet. And what we learned was that this was only the mid-way point to Everest Base Camp at 17,598 feet. And after base camp that's when the real mountain climbing began!

There is a picture I see in this. If you've been around church before then you may have heard the word justification. It means that despite your sin, God's judgment over you is "not guilty." Your sins and my sins have been paid for at the cross when Jesus bled and died for us. This is remarkable news! And this is only base camp.

What many of us have not yet heard or grasped is that the same God who sent his Son to die for you also adopts you as his very own child. Justification is base camp and the doctrine of adoption is Mount Everest, the summit of the gospel. The highest peak and the greatest privilege we have from God is to be his children. Scripture says, "See what kind of love the Father has given to us, that we should be called children of God; and so we are."[8] The kind of love God has for you is not only a love that declares you forgiven; it is the love of a perfect father for his kids. J.I. Packer explains it this way, "To be right with God the Judge is a great thing, but to be loved and cared for by God the Father is a greater."[9]

Most of us worry about money because we haven't climbed high enough in our grasp of the gospel. We know enough of God to be saved, but not enough to be free. We stop at base camp when Jesus offers us Everest.

---

8   1 John 3:1
9   J.I. Packer, Knowing God (Downers Grove, IL: InterVarsity Press, 1973), 207.

The Truest Thing About You

My friend Janice climbed Everest. It was neither fast, nor easy. In her twenties Janice lived the high-life in Manhattan, enjoying all that it offered: wealth, connections, cars, drivers, homes in the Hamptons and homes in California. But despite her success, deep down she had an anxiety about money that wouldn't go away. Janice tells her story this way:

"I think I was just buying into the security that I could provide by my zeros. And that just really isn't the truth so I was always worried. I was always anxious. My whole life, since I was a little girl, has been about living in this place of fear that it would all be gone after I made it. And I made and lost fortunes so that's happened to me. But once I really started believing that I was a daughter of the king, that God loved and delighted in me, and that he was never going to leave or forsake me, that's where this freedom came. I've had a security blanket all these years; I just didn't know it. That safety net is the loving arms of Jesus."

We are on an adventure to see ourselves this way. It's a journey that will finish when we are with Jesus in heaven, but for now it involves letting go of other ways we seek identity. It takes tenacity to believe God's words about you day after day after day. But this is a journey to freedom because at your core you are not a successful person or a failure, a wealthy person or a poor person, a creative or an athlete. Money doesn't define you. Your truest identity does not come from being praised by others. You are more than an artist or an accountant, a filmmaker or a financial advisor. These are roles you play for a season in life, but as Janice discovered, the truest thing about you is that you are a child of the living God.[10] At your core God delights in you.[11] You are precious in his eyes, honored and loved.[12] This might sound soft and fluffy to some of you, but I promise you this is rugged mountain climbing.

Jesus' brilliant antidote to our anxiety about money is hidden in his question, "Are you not of more value than the birds of the air?" I believe he waits for us to answer the question: Am I valuable to God?

The irony is that Jesus asks us this question, but he is the ultimate answer. Jesus' life and death are the proof that we are valuable to God. God loved us enough "that he gave his only Son, that whoever believes in him should not perish but have eternal life."[13] I cannot comprehend how much you would have to love someone to give your only son for them, but this is what our God does. There is nothing greater God could do to prove how much he values you.

If we don't believe we're valuable to God then we'll stress and worry. We'll strive to control our lives and secure our future. But once we believe deeply that God values us, this is where freedom enters in.

---

10   John 1:12
11   Isaiah 62:4
12   Isaiah 43:4
13   John 3:16

Putting it into Practice

For this training exercise you'll start by reading and discussing a few verses of Scripture with your team. Then there is an outline of what to do between now and the next time your group meets. Ultimately, this training exercise is about building a fresh foundation in your heart for a new relationship with God and money.[14]

14   The idea for this exercise was inspired by Dr. John Coe, Director of the Institute for Spiritual
     Formation at Talbot School of Theology, and his 'Prayer of Recollection', which you can read at:
     http://www.redeemerlm.org/uploads/1/2/0/7/12077040/prayer_of_recollection.pdf (viewed August
     28, 2018)

5-Day
Foundation

TRAINING EXERCISE 2

Step 1   Have three people each read one of these
verses aloud:

JOHN 1:12 (ESV)

But to all who did receive him, who believed in his name, he
gave the right to become children of God.

1 JOHN 3:1 (ESV)

See what kind of love the Father has given to us, that we should
be called children of God; and so we are.

ROMANS 8:15 (ESV)

For you did not receive the spirit of slavery to fall back into fear,
but you have received the Spirit of adoption as sons, by whom
we cry, "Abba! Father!"

Step 2   What do you notice? Which word or phrase most stands out to you? Take a couple minutes to write your thoughts down. Then share these among your team.

Step 3   Victory begins in identity. So for the next five mornings, your assignment is to pray two prayers at the beginning of your day that will help remind you of your true identity in Christ. The first is a prayer of release and you could pray something like this:

PRAYER OF RELEASE

Father in Heaven, I choose to believe you today that my identity is not found in being a successful person or a failure, in being wealthy or needy. At my core I am more than the roles I play, more than a father or a mother, a husband or a wife, a son or a daughter. God, I release to you my desire to base my identity in my performance or what other people say about me. In you, God, I am more than my career or calling, more than my abilities or accomplishments. I release to you all the ways I strive to find identity apart from you, Father. Please, bring me back to the truth of who you are and who I am.

The second prayer I invite you to pray over the next five mornings affirms the truth of who you are in Christ. You could pray something like this:

PRAYER OF RECEIVING

Father in Heaven, I affirm today that my highest and truest identity is in being your child.[15] Your word says I am valuable to you.[16] So valuable that you would send your Son Jesus into the world for me.[17] So valuable that Jesus would die for my sins.[18] Thank you, God for loving me that much.[19] Thank you that I am a new creation in Christ. The old has passed away; the new has come.[20] The truth is you delight in me and call me by name.[21] You say I am precious in your eyes, honored and loved.[22] Help me rise up into who you say that I am and truly live as a child of God.

Step 4   After praying, reread one of the Bible verses above and spend a few minutes thinking about it.

---

15   John 1:12
16   Matthew 6:26; Luke 12:7
17   1 John 4:9
18   Romans 5:8; 1 John 4:10
19   John 3:16
20   2 Corinthians 5:17
21   Isaiah 62:4; 43:1
22   Isaiah 43:4

Step 5   Journal: How was this experience for you? What did
you learn? What was God doing in your life?

_____

_____

_____

_____

_____

_____

THIS WEEK'S VIDEO:

givingtogether.video/identity

Remember that knowing our true identity in God is always
the foundation for all that we do, so this may be an exercise
you want to continue or come back to throughout our
adventure together.

Start Small

On my last birthday I sat down to open a few cards that came in the mail. The first was from my 86-year-old grandmother, and as I opened the envelope, out fell a five-dollar bill. My six-year-old son quickly snatched it up and asked, "Can I have it?"

"Sure, buddy," I replied. "But what do you want it for?"

"I want to buy you dinner," he said with a shy smile. "Is this enough for our whole family?"

"No, that's not enough."

Pulling out my wallet, I handed him a twenty-dollar bill.

"Is this enough for our whole family?" he asked again.

"No, that's not enough."

Again I put a twenty into his little hands.

"Is this enough for our whole family?"

"Yes, that should be enough."

My son proudly carried his little wallet stuffed with cash into the pizza restaurant where we would have dinner. When it came time to pay, I lifted him up so he could hand the money to the girl behind the cash register. My son was beaming.

At the table, my daughter said very sincerely, "Thank you, Malachi, for buying us dinner." My wife and I said the same, and the look on little Malachi's face was pure joy.

As we said back at base camp, generosity is a mindset – a mindset that leads to joy. No matter what age you are, you can develop this mindset and experience more joy.

Generosity = Happiness

The world has it upside down. Bigger, better, faster, newer is not the path to happiness. More stuff doesn't equal more joy. If you've ever traveled to a third world country, you've likely seen very poor people who are happier than everyone in your neighborhood. The question is: Why?

It's because the truth is the opposite of what we've been sold. The connection between money and happiness is not between having and happiness; it's between giving and happiness. Decades of research has consistently shown that generosity leads to greater happiness than if we spend money on ourselves.[1] I have a friend named Todd Harper who often says he has never met an unhappy generous person, and the data backs him up. Neuroscientists now say that the pleasure we receive from giving is hard-wired into our brains.[2] We're made to be givers.

But on average, American Christians give only two to three percent of their incomes to charity. Many give nothing at all. We work hard. We make money. And we keep it for ourselves, despite being the most affluent generation of Christians in history.

We're missing out on so much joy.

1   Harvard Business Review, "How Money Actually Buys Happiness", June 28, 2013: hbr.org/2013/06/how-money-actually-buys-happiness (viewed August 26, 2018); Nature Communications, "A Neural Link Between Generosity and Happiness", July 11, 2017: nature.com/articles/ncomms15964.pdf (viewed August 26, 2018); Time Magazine, "Being Generous Really Does Make You Happier", June 14, 2107: time.com/4857777/generosity-happiness-brain/ (viewed August 26, 2018)

2   Washington Post, "If It Feels Good to Be Good, It Might Be Only Natural", May 28, 2007: washingtonpost.com/wp-dyn/content/article/2007/05/27/AR2007052701056.html?noredirect=on (viewed August 25, 2018)

Radical Generosity Is Normal Christianity

Two thousand years ago Jesus talked about the joy of giving. He said famously, "It is more blessed to give than to receive."[3] A good synonym for the word 'blessed' is 'happy'. Jesus wants us to know that giving is the path to greater happiness.

When we look at the lives of the very first Christians, we see they understood and lived this out. The book of Acts tells us that "they were selling their possessions and belongings and distributing the proceeds to all, as any had need. And day by day, attending the temple together and breaking bread in their homes, they received their food with glad and generous hearts."[4]

These early believers lived out the words of Jesus. They focused more on giving than receiving and had great joy. Even when the first-century church grew to around 10,000 believers, their generosity DNA remained intact. The book of Acts practically repeats this description of their giving: we're told there was not a needy person among them! They even sold land and houses in order to give more![5]

Can you imagine that happening in your church? This sounds so radical to us, so different from how we live today. But what I've come to see is that radical generosity is normal Christianity.

The surprising first step in first-century giving wasn't a big missions offering. They didn't kick off a building campaign. Nor

---

3   Acts 20:35
4   Acts 2:45-46
5   Acts 4:32-35

did they rally to end poverty in Jerusalem. The first cause they gave to was each other. They met the needs of those in their church. Now I don't believe they abandoned all personal property rights, but instead that the generosity culture was so thick that when a need arose they knew that what's mine really is yours and what's yours really is mine.

To live this way the early church had to have grasped something we miss. But what?

The Core of Christianity

Perhaps Jesus' parable of the sheep and the goats was still fresh in their minds and they could still hear his words: "Truly, I say to you, as you did it to one of the least of these my brothers, you did it to me."[6] Maybe the apostle John was preaching what he later wrote down: "If anyone has the world's goods and sees his brother in need, yet closes his heart against him, how does God's love abide in him."[7]

But what they knew for sure was that Christianity, at its core, is good news. And this good news is of a generous God who has done something we never could have imagined he would do. He has given something we never would have dared to ask for.

The truth we have missed is that the gospel is generosity. We see in Scripture that God is the greatest of patrons, the giver of

---

6   Matthew 25:40
7   1 John 3:17

every good gift. He's the life-giver, who "gives to all mankind life and breath and everything."[8] He's the grace-giver, offering salvation as "the gift of God, not a result of works."[9] And he's also the victory-giver in whom "death is swallowed up in victory. O death, where is your victory? O death, where is your sting? The sting of death is sin, and the power of sin is the law. But thanks be to God, who gives us the victory through our Lord Jesus Christ."[10]

What do we have that we did not receive?[11] To be a Christian means you have received the generous love of God poured out in Jesus. To live as a Christian means we respond to God's generosity by no longer living for ourselves but for him who died and rose for us.[12] It's living to give instead of get, to lay down our lives instead of protect them.

What if we were the generation to recapture our faith in a generous God and begin to live it out? What if we each cultivated a heartbeat of generosity like God's? And what if our churches returned to first-century DNA and met one another's needs like family? It's time we see God again for who he is and take a step of faith in the direction of true joy.

---

8   Acts 17:25
9   Ephesians 2:8-9
10   1 Corinthians 15:54-57
11   1 Corinthians 4:7
12   2 Corinthians 5:15

It Starts with Each Other

As I led the first beta groups through *Giving Together*, I challenged them to start small and meet a need of someone in their local church. I didn't tell them how much to give or who to give to, but just to do something.

When we came back together that next week, Blake and Jackie, a young married couple, shared: "We were a little nervous about this exercise and didn't know who to give to. But then we thought of a family in our church who were adopting a child. We figured they would need financial help, so we wrote a check and put it in an envelope with a card. Then when we saw them at church on Sunday we didn't exactly know how to give it to them, so we just walked up to them while were talking with someone else and more or less threw the card at them and ran away." They laughed, "We were so awkward, but later on they found us and were so thankful, saying, 'We have needed to raise funds to help with our adoption expenses, but we didn't know how to talk about it. This is a big encouragement, knowing there are people out there who want to support us!'"

Another guy named Ryan shared that he felt God leading him to ask the youth director at church if there were any needs he could help with. As it turned out, two students needed help covering their costs to go to camp. Ryan was able to step in and do that and later reflected on it saying, "It wasn't a big need, but God was just looking for my obedience."

My own experience was that as I prayed about who God wanted me to give to only one name kept coming to mind: Jonathan. He was a young man in his mid-twenties in my church who was newly married and had significant student loans. I talked to my wife about it, we prayed together and wrote a check to give him and his wife on Sunday. After the service finished I said, "I know you feel the weight of your student loans and I wish I could take care of them all for you, but here's a little help so that you know you're not alone. We love you. God loves you. Keep trusting him." Tears streamed down his wife's face as they gave me hugs and thanked me. My joy soared.

As our *Giving Together* group wrapped up one evening, Andrew spoke up right at the end and said, "Growing up, my parents never did well for themselves financially. We were in the poor neighborhood in a very rich community. My parents lived there so I could go to the schools. But going to my church and seeing wealthy people come into church was part of what drove me away from the church. I never knew how those could be held in a paradigm. It's been a struggle for me. I think it's really important that we're doing this."

Fear or Faith

What we're attempting together is not easy. It's one thing to talk about giving and generosity, but any time you actually try to take action, you'll be met by an old friend named Fear. Fear will always promote a scarcity mentality, telling you to look out for yourself and play it safe. Fear will say there's not enough. You might even hear Fear's favorite diversion, "Do it later."

But if you're a follower of Jesus, then Fear is not your master anymore, "for God gave us a spirit not of fear but of power and love and self-control."[13] So I want you to listen to a better friend, one named Faith. Faith operates on the promises of God, not the principles of the world, reminding you that "one gives freely, yet grows all the richer; another withholds what he should give, and only suffers want."[14] Faith will remind you who you are and who your Father is. Faith's voice assures you that "God will supply every need of yours according to his riches in glory in Christ Jesus."[15]

In the end, who you listen to will determine how you act. Faith will lead you to joy. Fear will take you to anxiety. Faith is how we please God.[16] Fear is how Satan controls us. I've listened to both voices at different points in my life, and Fear has never left me with a good story to tell. But every step of Faith has led me further up and further in on the adventure with God. I want you to experience that adventure too and find, like the early church, that we really can be glad and generous.

Let's get started.

---

13   2 Timothy 1:7
14   Proverbs 11:24
15   Philippians 4:19 (see also Romans 8:31–32 and 2 Corinthians 9:8–11)
16   Hebrews 11:6

We Are
The Church
Experiment

TRAINING EXERCISE 3

We Are The Church Experiment

Step 1   As you begin, discuss your experience of Training Exercise 2 (5-Day Foundation). How was this exercise for you? What did you learn? What was difficult? What was God doing in your life?

Step 2   Read Acts 4:32-37 aloud.

ACTS 4:32-37 (ESV)

Now the full number of those who believed were of one heart and soul, and no one said that any of the things that belonged to him was his own, but they had everything in common. And with great power the apostles were giving their testimony to the resurrection of the Lord Jesus, and great grace was upon them all. There was not a needy person among them, for as many as were owners of lands or houses sold them and brought the proceeds of what was sold and laid it at the apostles' feet, and it was distributed to each as any had need. Thus Joseph, who was also called by the apostles Barnabas (which means son of encouragement), a Levite, a native of Cyprus, sold a field that belonged to him and brought the money and laid it at the apostles' feet.

Step 3   What do you notice from this passage? Which phrase or sentence most stands out to you? Take a few minutes to write down your thoughts and then share them with your team.

_____

_____

_____

Step 4   The early church started by giving to each other. Two thousand years later, we can do the same. Think about the church you're a part of. (If you're not a part of a church yet, prayerfully deciding to be a part of one is your training exercise.) Think about the people in your church. Who are the widows? Who are the single mothers? Who is sick or in the hospital? Who has recently lost a job?

Who is struggling under the weight of debt? Who are the college students? Who are the missionaries coming home for a break? Who needs some encouragement that God sees them? Write down a few names of people that come to mind:

Name 1 _____

Name 2 _____

Name 3 _____

Step 5   Pray and ask the Lord to show you one need you could meet or one person you could help.

Step 6   Decide if you want to give anonymously (Matthew 6:2-4) or openly (Acts 4:36-37). Both are biblical and can be a blessing in different ways.

Step 7   Do something. Success doesn't equal the perfect plan or a dramatic story to tell. Success is risking in the right direction for the right reason.

Step 8   Rehearse God's ability to meet your needs as you give to others. Read and meditate on one of these passages:

PHILIPPIANS 4:19

And my God will supply every need of yours according to his riches in glory in Christ Jesus.

2 CORINTHIANS 9:8

And God is able to make all grace abound to you, so that having all sufficiency in all things at all times, you may abound in every good work.

PROVERBS 11:24-25

One gives freely, yet grows all the richer; another withholds what he should give, and only suffers want.
Whoever brings blessing will be enriched, and one who waters will himself be watered.

Step 9   Journal: Who did God lead you to? What happened? What did you learn about God and about yourself?

_____

_____

_____

_____

_____

_____

_____

_____

_____

_____

_____

_____

THIS WEEK'S VIDEO:

givingtogether.video/start

Commit to Community

A man named David Blatt was brought in to northeast Ohio to coach a basketball team who, in their 45 years of existence, had never won a championship. But now they had one of the best players of all time and were closer than ever. The city of Cleveland was buzzing with excitement and expectation.

However, despite his initial success, Coach Blatt was fired after a year and a half because he was not good enough at one critical aspect of success. The team's General Manager explained in a press conference:

"We've been a group of tremendous individual talent with individual hopes and dreams. That's not a winning formula. We have to have group buy-in and team-first habits in order to become the team that we intend to be. And if we can do that, if we can learn to express collective greatness and the joy that brings, then we can dream about something more. Right now we're a really long way from that."[1]

The Cleveland Cavaliers hired a new head coach and within just a few months they went on to overcome impossible odds and win their first ever NBA championship. They didn't have any new players; they just finally had become a team.

Your Team

The hardest part about being a team is deciding to be one. Innately, we all look out for ourselves. We choose independence. We may have longings in our hearts to be a part of something bigger than ourselves, but when push comes to shove we go solo instead.

But solo isn't working. We need something more.

---

[1] nba.com/video/channels/nba_tv/2016/01/22/20160122-gt-griffin-on-blatt.nba/ (viewed August 28, 2018)

From the very beginning God said, "It is not good that the man should be alone; I will make him a helper fit for him."[2] God made Adam and Eve into the world's first team. There was perfect unity between them; the two became one flesh.[3]

Then when Jesus began his earthly ministry, he started another kind of team. It originated as the size of a basketball team: twelve young guys with a mix of backgrounds and personalities. Soon it grew to include a broader network of men and women, who together formed the foundation of a new kind of team that Jesus called the church. Church was meant to be more than a building; more than a 90-minute service on Sundays. Church is a united team of people who are following Jesus and learning to obey everything he commanded.

God saves us as individuals, but he doesn't leave us that way. For every follower of Jesus, the church is your team and God is your coach. God is constantly molding his followers to be an elite team. We can push against this and remain a collection of individuals, or we can opt in and be a team. This choice cuts against the grain of our nature and culture, but it is the winning formula.

---

2   Genesis 2:18

3   Genesis 2:24

Your Decision

A decade after Jesus' death, resurrection and ascension into heaven, the early church faced this choice. They had expanded beyond Jerusalem into Asia and Europe and in those days, God warned them "that there would be a great famine over all the world."[4] The food shortage was especially going to impact the region of Judea. Judea was where their team began. Jesus was from Judea. It's where he started preaching. John the Baptist also began in Judea. What would the wider church do in Judea's time of need?

The Bible tells us that "the disciples determined, every one according to his ability, to send relief to the brothers living in Judea."[5]

The disciples "determined." They decided. They chose. The church wasn't going to be like the world where everyone looked out for themselves alone. They committed to be different, to sacrifice for one another.

This wasn't a decision anyone was forced into. It wasn't a law they were keeping or a percentage they were obligated to give. This was a commitment to one another, a decision they made, "everyone according to his ability."

Generosity often begins as a reaction. We get a letter in the mail. The church announces they're behind budget. The missionary has needs. We are invited to a dinner or a donor weekend. But what would it look like if we didn't simply react, but determined to be

---

4   Acts 11:28
5   Acts 11:29

givers? Have you and I made up our minds not just to go to church, but to be the church?

When the apostle Paul taught the Corinthian church about giving, he wrote: "Each one must give as he has decided in his heart..."[6] Giving begins with a decision. That decision acknowledges that our money has been given to us by God for his purposes.[7] Some of it is for our needs, but not all of it. God entrusts us with wealth that we might pursue his purposes on earth. Giving isn't a tip or a tax we pay God. It's not a bargaining chip to make God bless us or answer our prayers. Instead, giving is an offering and an opportunity.

First, giving is an offering back to God a portion of what he has given to us.[8] Giving says, "Thank you." Giving says, "I trust you." Giving says, "This stuff doesn't control me." Second, giving is an opportunity to bless the world. Giving makes a contribution. Giving meets the real needs of real people. Giving connects vision with provision so that God's kingdom advances.

What we see in the early church is that every one gave "according to his ability."[9] Some could give more. Some less. But each one decided to do what they could with what they had.

Too often we fail to give what we can because we're looking at others' ability instead of our own. We fall back into thinking generosity is an amount, a check with a lot of zeros behind it, not a mindset. But the way of the early church was to give as they'd been given

---

6   2 Corinthians 9:7
7   Deuteronomy 8:18
8   1 Chronicles 29:14
9   Acts 11:29

to. They focused on what they could do, not on what others could or should do.

Together they sent relief 300 miles away "...to the brothers."[10] They knew the church in Judea was family. This was their team. According to Scripture, God's team is the church and the church is his family. This makes every other Christian your brother or sister. And as the early church knew, "if one member suffers, all suffer together; if one member is honored, all rejoice together."[11]

Your Leaders

"How does this apply to us?" you may be asking. "If I gave to my church, much of it would go to paying pastors' salaries. Does the Bible say anything about that?"

Yes. The theme we see throughout the Bible is that those who care for us spiritually are to receive financial provision. In the Old Testament, God chose one tribe out of the people of Israel to be priests who served at the sanctuary and performed sacrifices on behalf of all God's people. The Levites were these spiritual leaders and God's command to the other eleven tribes was to give a tenth of their income to them. God said, "To the Levites I have given every tithe in Israel for an inheritance, in return for their service that they do."[12]

---

10   Acts 11:29
11   1 Corinthians 12:26
12   Numbers 18:21

God also used a metaphor to instruct us in this, saying, "You shall not muzzle an ox when it is treading out the grain."[13] The New Testament helps us interpret this by asking: "Is it for oxen that God is concerned? Does he not certainly speak for our sake? It was written for our sake, because the plowman should plow in hope and the thresher thresh in hope of sharing in the crop. If we have sown spiritual things among you, is it too much if we reap material things from you?"[14]

The summary of the New Testament's teaching is this: "The Lord commanded that those who proclaim the gospel should get their living by the gospel."[15] Those who lead the church are worthy of our financial support.[16] Scripture says, "Let the one who is taught the word share all good things with the one who teaches."[17]

Most pastors have not taken a vow of poverty. It's not in their job descriptions to struggle financially. Instead, it's in our job description to provide for their needs. God wants his church to be an elite team where those who lead are supported, those in need are provided for, and everyone is generous.

But I know you and I can be hesitant or even skeptical to give when we've heard stories of spiritual leaders mishandling money or living lavish lifestyles. This is nothing new. In Jesus' day he saved his strongest words for the religious leaders who loved money. Jesus said (I can imagine him yelling): "Woe to you, scribes and

---

13   Deuteronomy 25:4
14   1 Corinthians 9:9–11
15   1 Corinthians 9:14
16   1 Timothy 5:17
17   Galatians 6:6

Pharisees, hypocrites! For you clean the outside of the cup and the plate, but inside they are full of greed and self-indulgence."[18] Our God does not deal lightly with greedy spiritual leaders.

The apostle Paul wrote that godly leaders must not be lovers of money or greedy.[19] Peter also wrote that money must never be the motivation for ministry. Instead, pastors must "shepherd the flock of God that is among you, exercising oversight, not under compulsion, but willingly, as God would have you; not for shameful gain."[20]

My friend Mart gives extravagantly to church and ministry and his helpful paradigm is to look for leaders with 'GHI': generosity, humility and integrity. Mart says, "I believe these three character traits are the antidote to the three tricks of Satan, which are lust of the eyes, pride of life and lust of the flesh. If you find someone with GHI they are on their way to conquering the tricks of the devil and doing great things for the glory of God."

Pastors are to receive generosity but they are also called to lead in generosity. Jesus wants leaders who practice what they preach and a church family who strongly supports them. Unity is our road to victory.

I hope by now you're experiencing the benefits of having a team for your *Giving Together* journey. Your next training exercise will be a chance to decide. I can barely imagine the blessing to pastors and churches around the world if you and I not only read this chapter, but also put it into practice.

---

18   Matthew 23:25; see also Luke 11:39-40
19   1 Timothy 3:3, 8
20   1 Peter 5:2

90-Day
Giving
Challenge

TRAINING EXERCISE 4

90-Day
Giving
Challenge

Step 1 As you begin, discuss your experience of Training Exercise 3 (We Are The Church Experiment). How was this exercise for you? What did you learn? What was difficult? What was God doing in your life?

Step 2 Read 2 Corinthians 9:6–8 aloud.

2 CORINTHIANS 9:6–8

The point is this: whoever sows sparingly will also reap sparingly, and whoever sows bountifully will also reap bountifully. Each one must give as he has decided in his heart, not reluctantly or under compulsion, for God loves a cheerful giver. And God is able to make all grace abound to you, so that having all sufficiency in all things at all times, you may abound in every good work.

Step 3   What do you notice from this passage? Which phrase or sentence most stands out to you? Write it down.

_____

_____

_____

Step 4   This exercise is to pray and decide on a 90-day giving goal for your church. How much money do you think Jesus wants you to give to your church over the next three months?

Step 5   Some of you may sense that God is asking you to give like the Macedonians out of your "extreme poverty" (2 Corinthians 8:2). Others may feel invited to "excel" in giving like never before (2 Corinthians 8:7). For everyone, this assignment is the hard work of prayerfully deciding.

Step 6   Write down your giving goal:

_____

Step 7   Decide how often you'll give: every week, every two
weeks, once a month or all at once.

_____

Step 8   Start giving!

Step 9   <u>Journal:</u> What was challenging about this
assignment? How did God lead you? What was
God doing in your life?

_____

_____

_____

_____

_____

THIS WEEK'S VIDEO:

givingtogether.video/community

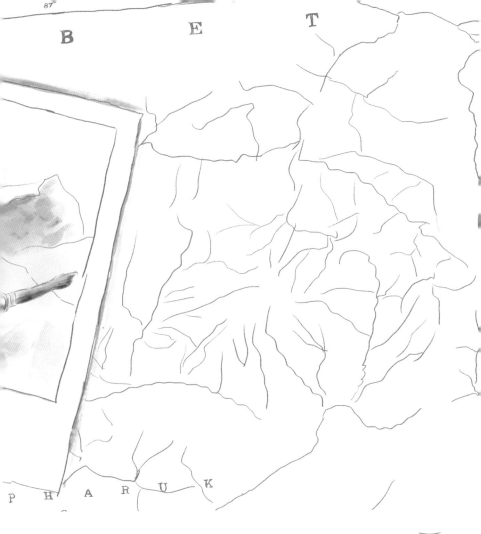

Redefine Rewards

I wanted to be rich, so rich that I could buy my parents a house the size of the school administration building across the street from our town home. From a young age I thought that more money meant you were winning and a big house equaled success.

Each of us has a mental picture of where we think we could be or should be. My picture was playing professional baseball for the Minnesota Twins and having enough money to buy my parents a huge house. My friend Caleb wanted to be like Coach Joe, a successful lawyer, who coached little league and used to buy pizza for the whole team after their games. My wife saw herself living in a New York City apartment with an exposed brick wall and a cat.

What's your picture? It might be based off of your parents, an older brother or sister or a character you saw in a movie. My friend Henry says, "I watched the movie *Wall Street* and you remember Charlie Sheen's character Bud Fox? He's got two phones, he's dating Daryl Hannah, he's got the apartment on the Upper West Side and he has his own sushi maker. I wanted to be that guy."

We all have some image in our minds of what success looks like, some mental bull's-eye that we're aiming our lives at. One of the most import decisions you could make in life is to honestly acknowledge that picture and then ask: Is my bull's-eye what God wants me to aim at?

Something is Missing

Two thousand years ago a young man came to Jesus and was given just this opportunity. His mental picture was exposed, and he was faced with the hardest decision of his life: Am I willing to redefine my picture of success?

He was a guy who had been successful early in life. He was a high achiever. Rich. Respected in the community. Used to being thought of as a good guy. But something ached in his soul for more, and he believed Jesus had the answer.

So one day he ran up to Jesus, knelt before him and asked, "Good Teacher, what must I do to inherit eternal life?"[1]

He knew something was missing. It was something money couldn't buy. But perhaps it was something he could achieve if only he knew what it was. So he asked Jesus, "What must I do?"

Jesus responds with a challenge, saying, "Why do you call me good? No one is good except God alone."[2]

The rich young ruler didn't believe Jesus was God and he wasn't looking for grace. What he wanted was advice. He wanted self-help for redeeming his own life. I can almost hear him saying, "If there's a deed, I'll do it. If there's a test, I'll pass it. If there's a challenge, I'll conquer it. I'm a pretty good guy."

But Jesus continues, "You know the commandments: 'Do not murder, Do not commit adultery, Do not steal, Do not bear false witness, Do not defraud, Honor your father and mother.'"[3]

On the surface it looks like Jesus plays his game, saying, "Oh, you want something to do? Have you considered God's Ten Commandments? How about commandments five through nine?"

And the young man thinks he passed this test. "Teacher," he said,

1   Mark 10:17
2   Mark 10:18
3   Mark 10:19

"all these I have kept from my youth."[4] He's pretty happy about his performance. He seems to be saying, "Jesus, don't you see what a good boy I've been? I'm not violent. I don't steal or lie. I'm faithful to my wife and honor my parents."

But deep down something is still missing. The rich young ruler hasn't yet seen that God doesn't simply want us to be morally upright; he wants us to worship him. The Ten Commandments don't start with us and our behavior; they start with God. Commandment number one is, "You shall have no other gods before me" and this is the one thing the rich young ruler was not prepared to do.[5]

The bulls-eye for his life didn't even include God. Religion, yes. Commandments, some of them. Making money, absolutely. But God? Jesus wanted to expose his mental picture and show him that this vision of success was not success at all.

I find this story so challenging because in the rich young ruler I see myself. Like him I can believe that what I really need is advice, not grace. If only I knew the right things to do, then I would be able to fix what's wrong with my life. I too think I can be successful on my own if only I work harder. After all, I'm a pretty good guy. I'm not violent. I don't steal or lie. I'm faithful to my wife and honor my parents. But this is the same sin as Adam and Eve who thought, "I can have life without God."

---

4   Mark 10:20
5   Exodus 20:3

The Trade-Off

Into these dark places in our hearts, Jesus speaks. The story continues: "And Jesus, looking at him, loved him, and said to him, 'You lack one thing: go, sell all that you have and give to the poor, and you will have treasure in heaven; and come, follow me.' "[6]

First, we see that Jesus loved him. Oh, what a glorious line! Despite the rich young ruler's striving and independence, he was loved. Jesus didn't expect him to be perfect. He didn't shame or condemn him. Jesus loved him and lovingly offered him a rare invitation.

Second, Jesus offered him a second chance; an opportunity to start over with the first commandment. Jesus said to him, "Follow me." These exact words were how Jesus called his first followers. Four fishermen – Andrew, Peter, James and John – were also invited to leave their definition of success, which was their nets, their boats and their income, and redefine their lives with God in the center. This same offer came to the rich young ruler. He too could join Jesus' band of followers, travel with them, witness miracles, hear Jesus' teaching, get the private explanations of his parables and, most of all, walk with the Son of God. Jesus' invitation was to a great adventure of faith.

Third, we see Jesus' invitation came with an astounding promise: "Go, sell all that you have and give to the poor, *and you will have treasure in heaven.*"

---

6   Mark 10:21

If you've heard this story before you've probably thought to yourself, "I'm glad Jesus didn't command me to sell everything." But what we miss is that Jesus was not trying to take away from the rich young ruler but give him something infinitely greater. The call to sell everything was not a loss, but an exchange. Jesus was offering him the chance to trade in earthly treasure for heavenly treasure. This was an opportunity for the rich young ruler to invest his money in a currency that would never fluctuate and into an economy that would never fail. It was a chance to bank with Jesus where moth and rust do not destroy and thieves do not break in and steal.

We don't talk much about eternal rewards or treasure in heaven, but this was exactly how Jesus sought to motivate the rich young ruler. Think about what Jesus could have said instead:

"Go, sell all that you have and give to the poor because their needs are so great and you have the ability to do something about it."

Or Jesus could have said, "Go, sell all that you have and give to the poor because that would be the loving thing to do."

Or, "Go, sell all that you have and give to the poor because it's your duty to share with those in need."

Or even, "Go, sell all that you have and give to the poor because your generosity would reflect and glorify God."

But none of those are what Jesus said. Instead, Jesus appealed to the young man's self-interest, offering him treasure in heaven in return for giving his treasure on earth.

Driven by Rewards

At this point you're probably wondering, "But isn't it selfish to seek our own rewards?" That would be a great question for my kids who did a summer reading program through our city library. I've never seen them so driven to read. They started as soon as they woke up and were reading when I came home from work because they knew their reward from the library would be a gift card for free tacos. And my kids really like to eat. Is that selfish?

Or we could ask a friend of mine who is a speech therapist. She recently told me that if she takes on additional clients, her boss will give her half of the fees that come in. She was thrilled and plans to work a little harder for that bonus. Is that selfish?

Every four years the world loves to watch the Olympics and I've never heard anyone criticize the athletes for pursuing gold medals. Nobody says Usain Bolt or Michael Phelps should have slowed down to let other people win the gold instead. We all implicitly understand that rewards can drive us to be our best; they call us to do hard things in light of long-term gain. Olympic champions are those rare few who do what is hard over and over again. They train when others sleep. They say goodbye to temporary pleasures in pursuit of one great reward. We don't pity Olympic athletes; we admire them.

We are people driven by rewards. God wired us this way. It's why we use rewards cards and track our airline miles. It's why businessmen compete and entrepreneurs innovate. Many of you are geniuses at finding deals and discounts. Others of you happily work overtime because you get rewarded with time and half. I have friends who maximize their vacation days and paid time off like they're solving a calculus problem. I don't think any of these things are inherently selfish or wrong. There's a difference between healthy self-interest and selfishness.

Heaven is my Reward

Some of you are probably thinking what I have often thought: "Just getting into heaven and seeing Jesus is enough of a reward for me. I don't need treasure in heaven or a crown or anything else." But what I've come to see is that to say "Heaven is my reward" is actually not the gospel. Heaven is not a reward; it's a gift. As Ephesians 2 says, salvation "is not your own doing; it is the gift of God, not a result of works."[7] Heaven was purchased for us by Jesus' death on the cross. It's his gift to give. That means if you confess Jesus as your Savior and Lord then heaven is your base package, but commissions are also available. Forgiveness is totally free, but rewards are the result of faith-filled action.

Jesus knows that it's not a question of if we will seek rewards, but rather which rewards we will seek. The rewards of earth or the rewards of heaven. The rewards of man or the rewards of God. Rewards that last 30 years or rewards that last forever.

---

7   Ephesians 2:8–9

The Offer Still Stands

The rich young ruler made his choice. He settled for what was right in front of him instead of long-term gain. He had to have his money. He could not and would not redefine his picture of success. His story finished with this sad conclusion: "Disheartened by the saying, he went away sorrowful, for he had great possessions."[8]

But imagine if it had ended differently. What if he had said yes to Jesus instead of no? Then we may have known Jesus to have thirteen disciples instead of twelve. Perhaps the rich young ruler would have been used by God to write one of the books of the New Testament like Peter, James and John. Perhaps the rich young ruler would have had a prominent role in the book of Acts, spreading the gospel in Jerusalem, Judea, Samaria and to the ends of the earth. Perhaps God would have given him a ministry to others who had wealth, helping them to see it in light of eternity too. Perhaps.

We'll never know how the rich young ruler's story might have ended, but we can know how our own stories can end. Two thousand years later Jesus' offer still stands. No, we won't get to walk with Peter, James and John, but if we're willing to redefine success on God's terms and not our own, then an incredible adventure awaits, which will end in an eternity of rewards. If we decide to say yes to Jesus and leave behind anything he asks us to leave, then God will undoubtedly write a better story for our lives than we could ever write ourselves. The story of the rich young ruler teaches us that no matter what Jesus asks of us, following him is never a loss; it's always a gain.

---

8   Mark 10:22

The Rich
Young Ruler
Experience

TRAINING EXERCISE 5

The Rich Young Ruler Experience

Step 1   As you begin, discuss your experience of Training Exercise 4 (90-Day Giving Challenge). How was this exercise for you? What did you learn? What was difficult? What was God doing in your life?

Step 2   Pray as a team, asking God to help you fulfill your giving goals.

Step 3   Read Mark 10:17–31 aloud.

MARK 10:17–31

And as he was setting out on his journey, a man ran up and knelt before him and asked him, "Good Teacher, what must I do to inherit eternal life?" And Jesus said to him, "Why do you call me good? No one is good except God alone. You know the commandments: 'Do not murder, Do not commit adultery, Do not steal, Do not bear false witness, Do not defraud, Honor your father and mother.'" And he said to him, "Teacher, all these I have kept from my youth." And Jesus, looking at him, loved him, and said to him, "You lack one thing: go, sell all that you have and give to the poor, and you will have treasure in heaven; and come, follow me." Disheartened by the saying, he went away sorrowful, for he had great possessions.

And Jesus looked around and said to his disciples, "How difficult it will be for those who have wealth to enter the kingdom of God!" And the disciples were amazed at his words. But Jesus said to them again, "Children, how difficult it is to enter the kingdom of God! It is easier for a camel to go through the eye of a needle than for a rich person to enter the kingdom of God." And they were exceedingly astonished, and said to him, "Then who can be saved?" Jesus looked at them and said, "With man it is impossible, but not with God. For all things are possible with God." Peter began to say to him, "See, we have left everything and followed you." Jesus said, "Truly, I say to you, there is no one who has left house or brothers or sisters or mother or father or children or lands, for my sake and for the gospel, who will not receive a hundredfold now in this time, houses and brothers and sisters and mothers and children and lands, with persecutions, and in the age to come eternal life. But many who are first will be last, and the last first."

Step 4   What do you notice from this passage? Which phrase or sentence most stands out to you? Write it down and then share with your team.

_____

_____

_____

_____

_____

Step 5   Spend a few minutes thinking about your own mental picture of success. Who is this picture based on? Write it down and then share with your team.

_____

_____

_____

Step 6   What would it have been like for the rich young ruler to obey Jesus? I want you to experience this in a small way. Your assignment is to sell one thing you have and give the money you make to the poor.

Step 7   Pray and ask Jesus what you should sell. There's no rule here on what to sell or how valuable it should be. But you should make sure that you give out of your possessions, not your bank account.

Step 8   Write down anything the Lord brings to mind and your first ideas of what you could sell.

_____

_____

_____

_____

Step 9   Once you have decided on an item, sell it as soon as possible. Procrastination is the enemy of progress. Four apps that may be helpful for selling things online are Letgo, eBay, OfferUp and Mercari.

Step 10   Give the proceeds to the poor. If your church has a ministry to serve the poor or a deacon's fund that helps the needy, you may want to give that way. You could also partner with a Christian ministry in your city that serves the poor. Globally, there are many Christian organizations who care for the poor in a variety of ways: providing clean water, education, food, child sponsorship, disaster relief. Whatever you do, do something. Success doesn't equal the perfect plan or a dramatic story to tell. Success is risking in the right direction for the right reason.

Step 11   Read Proverbs 19:17 and reread Mark 10:21 to rehearse God's amazing promises.

PROVERBS 19:17

Whoever is generous to the poor lends to the Lord, and he will repay him for his deed.

MARK 10:21

And Jesus, looking at him, loved him, and said to him, "You lack one thing: go, sell all that you have and give to the poor, and you will have treasure in heaven; and come, follow me."

Step 12   Journal: What did you sell and how did you sell it?
How did you give the proceeds to the poor? What
was difficult? What was God doing in your life?

_____

_____

_____

_____

_____

_____

_____

THIS WEEK'S VIDEO:

givingtogether.video/rewards

Practice Partnership

We had just returned from visiting some missionary friends in India when my wife said, "We should support them."

"I just finished seminary," I replied. "And I don't have a job!"

My wife patiently smiled and said, "We saw their ministry up close. We believe in what they are doing and know they have financial needs."

"But when you start supporting someone on a monthly basis it could be a 30-year commitment," I continued. "That freaks me out. What if we start and then have to stop because we don't have the money?"

Renée stayed cheerful, neither arguing nor nagging me. Then one day God spoke to my heart with a clear and powerful thought that I knew I didn't come up with. He said: "If you are not going to support them, you're not going to support anyone. Your heart is either going to grow bigger and wider or get smaller, colder, darker and harder."

This thought scared me. This was no longer about money; it was about my heart. And the last thing I wanted was a small, cold, dark, hard heart.

"Fine!" I told Renée. "We're in for $100 a month. I don't know where the money is going to come from, but we're in."

This was my first big jump into giving and it felt as crazy as getting flung out of an airplane. A little while later I met three women who showed me that this is the way God works.

Three Women You Should Know

I was reading the Bible when a question popped into my head that I had never considered before. The question was: How did Jesus and his disciples fund their three years of ministry?

Jesus was 30 when he started his public ministry of preaching and teaching and healing people. Before then he was a carpenter, four of his disciples were fishermen, and one was a tax collector. They all left their jobs to go from town to town and village to village preaching. Surely they still had expenses. After all, they had to eat.

I must have assumed that God used miraculous means. God could have provided for Jesus in any number of ways:

God could have chosen for Jesus to be born into a wealthy family as a first-century trust-fund baby who never had any needs. That would have lightened the load in ministry, but that's not what God did.

God could have commanded Jesus to miraculously multiply baskets of fish and loaves of bread every day for lunch for him and his disciples. They could have hung on to the baskets of leftovers for dinner.[1] But that's not what God did.

Jesus could have bank rolled ministry by repeatedly turning water into wine and setting up the best winery in the Roman Empire.[2] I'm sure there would have been good money in the wine that Jesus was producing, but that's not how God provided.

Jesus could have started the world's greatest fishing business by telling his disciples where to drop their nets each morning in order to bring in huge catches of fish.[3] They could have pulled in such huge volumes of fish and sold their catches at great discounts that they would have dominated the market. But that's not what God did.

---

1   Mark 6:35–44, 8:1–9
2   John 2:1–10
3   Luke 5:4–7; John 21:4–8

Jesus could have instructed Peter to go catch more fish with coins in their mouths.[4] One coin to pay taxes, two to fund ministry, and it would have been easy.

But instead of any of these miraculous means, what I saw in Scripture was three women – Mary, Joanna and Susanna – who gave their wealth to provide for Jesus and his disciples. Luke 8:1–3 tells their story:

> *Soon afterward he [Jesus] went on through cities and villages, proclaiming and bringing the good news of the kingdom of God. And the twelve were with him, and also some women who had been healed of evil spirits and infirmities: Mary, called Magdalene, from whom seven demons had gone out, and Joanna, the wife of Chuza, Herod's household manager, and Susanna, and many others, who provided for them out of their means.*

God's method of providing for his Son was to call three women to be partners in the work through giving. Mary, Joanna and Susanna encountered Jesus' healing "of evil spirits and infirmities" and their lives were forever changed. Their response was to step forward and give so that more and more people could come to know the Jesus they loved. Imagine the return on that investment!

---

4   Matthew 17:24–27

True Partners

As we follow these three women through the Gospel of Luke, we see that they didn't simply give a gift and disappear. Mary, Joanna and Susanna continued to meet the needs of Jesus and his disciples from chapter eight all the way to chapter twenty-three, where Luke writes that "the women who had followed him from Galilee stood at a distance watching these things."[5] They were there at Jesus' crucifixion.

When Jesus' dead body was taken down from the cross, "the women who had come with him from Galilee followed and saw the tomb and how his body was laid. Then they returned and prepared spices and ointments."[6] Even after his death, these generous women were still providing for Jesus!

They were the first to go to Jesus' tomb on Sunday morning. They were the first to see the stone rolled away.[7] They were the first to hear from the angels that Jesus had risen.[8] And "Mary Magdalene and Joanna and Mary the mother of James and the other women with them" were the ones who told these things to the apostles.[9]

What a glorious role Mary, Joanna and Susanna had in the ministry of Jesus. They were real partners, invested and involved in Jesus' ministry to proclaim the gospel. I call them Jesus' Gospel Patrons.

The pattern we see in Scripture is that when God raises up

---

5   Luke 23:49
6   Luke 23:55–56
7   Luke 24:2
8   Luke 24:4–7
9   Luke 24:10

preachers and missionaries, he also raises up patrons to come alongside them.[10] They play different positions, but they're members of the same team.

I want you to see that you don't have to be somebody else to serve God. I've talked with businessmen whose growing faith has led them to consider leaving their careers to become pastors. But most have not yet seen the amazing part they can play with the gifts that God has already given them. You might be called to preach and teach. God might want to use you as a missionary. But Mary, Joanna and Susanna didn't miss their calling. They did exactly what God created them to do.

Sometimes God uses miraculous means to provide, but usually we are God's chosen method to provide for the work he wants done on earth. Some will speak and some will support. Some will go and others will give. Some will preach and many will provide. Giving is not something small or insignificant. It's right at the center of how God works in this world.

Lord willing, we will be the generation to take the good news of Jesus to every tribe and people and nation on earth. Lord willing, we will be the generation to translate the Bible into every remaining language. Lord willing, we will be the generation to start new churches in the global cities and rural villages of the world. And Lord willing, we will be the generation to see God work great and mighty revivals in our own cities and churches. For all of this we will need an army of Gospel Patrons who are prepared for

---

10   For further stories and examples, you can read Gospel Patrons (gospelpatrons.org).

partnership. People who aim for collective greatness. People like Mary, Joanna and Susanna.

One Powerful Question

It's been eight years since we decided to partner with our friends in India and, as you would expect, God has faithfully provided for us. Our partnership has become sweeter and their ministry has prospered. It's been a joy to play a small part in God's work through their lives, despite living 8,000 miles away.

God has kept the word he spoke to me eight years ago. My heart has been strengthened to take even greater steps of faith and now our family supports our local church on a monthly basis along with missionaries in Italy, Ethiopia, Kenya, Indonesia, Chad and Nepal. Our hearts have certainly grown larger and larger.

In our initial *Giving Together* groups, I challenged us to practice partnership by asking one question that 99 percent of pastors and ministry leaders have never been asked and 99 percent of us have never thought to ask them. It's a powerful question that can ignite partnerships and accomplish great purposes. It's not an easy question to ask or to answer, but I believe if more of us asked it, the world would change.

Because we asked this question, new ministries got funded and pastors were provided for. Churches found new church buildings to rent, pastors were able to strengthen their marriages and partnerships between ministry leaders and marketplace leaders grew.

This next training exercise is your chance to play offense with your giving. You don't have to wait for a need to arise. You don't have to wait for someone to ask for support. Instead, you can initiate and ask one powerful question that may forever change your life.

Ask It
Exercise

TRAINING EXERCISE 6

Ask It
Exercise

Step 1   As you begin, discuss your experience of Training
Exercise 5 (The Rich Young Ruler Experience).
How was this exercise for you? What did you
learn? What was difficult? What was God doing in
your life?

Step 2   Read Luke 8:1-3 aloud.

LUKE 8:1-3 (ESV)

Soon afterward he went on through cities and villages,
proclaiming and bringing the good news of the kingdom of
God. And the twelve were with him, and also some women
who had been healed of evil spirits and infirmities: Mary, called
Magdalene, from whom seven demons had gone out, and
Joanna, the wife of Chuza, Herod's household manager, and
Susanna, and many others, who provided for them out of
their means.

Step 3: What do you notice from this passage? Which phrase or sentence most stands out to you? Write it down.

_____

_____

_____

_____

Step 4 Your assignment is to think of a pastor, a missionary or a ministry leader you know and ask them this powerful question:

"What's one thing that would completely transform your ministry this year and set you up for success?"

So who would you want to ask?

Name _____

Step 5 They may need time to think about their answer. That's normal. But as you ask them, try to communicate your care for them and your willingness to listen to them without judgment no matter what their answer is. At times it can be hard for pastors and spiritual leaders to admit their needs and receive help because they are so used to caring for others. So show them you care. Write down their answer. Tell them you'll be praying for God to help you know how to respond.

Answer:

_____

_____

Step 6 Do something. Success doesn't equal the perfect plan or a dramatic story to tell. Success is risking in the right direction for the right reason.

Step 7 Read Philippians 4:19 and rehearse God's ability to meet your needs as you give to others.

PHILIPPIANS 4:19 (ESV)

And my God will supply every need of yours according to his riches in glory in Christ Jesus.

Step 8 <u>Journal:</u> What did God lead you to do? What did you learn? What was God doing in your life?

_____

_____

_____

_____

_____

_____

_____

_____

THIS WEEK'S VIDEO:

givingtogether.video/partnership

Intend Impact

Our team had finished producing four short films telling stories of generosity when we noticed a theme that ran through each one. It wasn't something we scripted, just something that was there. The theme was that each person we filmed had a defining moment of faith when they were out of their country and out of their comfort zone.

For Kevin and Leslie, it was on their trip to Dubai.

For Mart Green, it was his experience in Guatemala.

For Todd and Susan, it was a visit to a village in Tanzania.

For Ed, it happened while traveling around India.

Something woke up in all of their hearts when they saw the great needs of the world and recognized that God had put them in positions of influence and affluence for a reason.

It's astounding to stop and think that God, in his perfect wisdom, chose for you and me to live in this place and at this time. You could have been born in the Amazon jungle or in the Himalayan Mountains – but you weren't. You could have been born in the Middle Ages or biblical times – but you weren't. The two things that influence your life the most, the time and place of your birth, God decided for you.

The question for each of us is: Why?

Esther Still Speaks

There was a woman in the 5th century B.C. who had to wrestle with this very question. She was living in the capital city of Persia, which is modern-day Iran, and through an unusual set of circumstances she became the new queen. This young Jewish woman was now married to King Xerxes I, a man who ruled over 127 provinces from India to Ethiopia.

But when her husband's evil advisor Haman convinced him to make an irrevocable decree that all Jews in his kingdom be annihilated, Esther was caught between a rock and a hard place. If she did nothing, all of her people would die. But she also knew that in that culture she was not allowed to approach the king in his inner court. If she did, she could be the one put to death.

Life was comfortable and easy for her in the palace. She had servants, attendants and everything she ever needed. Why should she, the queen, risk her own life? And yet if she didn't, she was risking the lives of all of her people.

It was in this critical hour when her cousin Mordecai spoke to her the words you and I need to hear as well. He said: "And who knows whether you have not come to the kingdom for such a time as this?"[1]

This was Esther's hour. It was the reason she had been given so much favor, the reason she had been put in her position. She didn't know how her story would end, but she did know this was the biggest moment of her life.

We can identify with Esther. We often miss why we're here and what we're supposed to do with our lives. We lose focus. We drift. We settle. Many in our generation are caught up in endlessly entertaining themselves. We pursue pleasure, experiences and success, but can't find purpose. There's nothing that makes our blood boil. No great plans we're attempting. Nothing we are willing to live for and die for. And Ester still speaks.

Mordecai's words woke her up and Esther's response was to call all the Jews in her city to fast and pray for her for three days. After

---

1   Esther 4:14

that time, she said, "Then I will go to the king, though it is against the law, and if I perish, I perish."[2]

Sometimes all it takes to spring out of bed in the morning is to roll over and check the clock. The same is true spiritually. Once we know what time it is, our purpose becomes clear.

So what time is it? I'd like to make a case that we are living in the greatest time to be alive. I believe, in a very real sense, you and I have come into the kingdom for such a time as this.

What Time Is It?

In our generation there is a great hunger for more – more than the American Dream, more than safe and comfortable lives, more than retirement and golf. We're discontent with the status quo. We are a generation of dreamers, entrepreneurs and creatives. We are people who want our work to matter, to count for something more than a paycheck. We want to make an impact in the world. And now is the time.

Through the travel available to us, you can get to almost any place in the world in 24 hours. Through the technology available to us, you can spread a message around the world in a matter of seconds. Our world is global and connected.

In America, we are following the wealthiest generation in US history, which means our generation has had unprecedented

---

2   Esther 4:16

access to education. But we've also seen that money isn't every-thing. It doesn't solve all our problems. It's not the ultimate goal. We want more.

And into our generation, Jesus Christ speaks, offering us a global mission to be a part of. Jesus says, "You will be my witnesses in Je-rusalem, and in all Judea and Samaria, and to the end of the earth."[3]

God is writing a big story and he invites you to play a part. You can try to write your own little story, one that lasts 70 or 80 years and ends with a secure retirement, a comfortable chair and 162 channels on TV. Or you can join the greatest story ever told. You can watch the news or go out and make the news. I want to help you believe that you – yes, you – can make an impact. And it doesn't begin with finding your passion or determining your destiny. It be-gins by seeing, like Esther did, that amidst incredible challenges God is in control and he has positioned you perfectly to step out in faith and join him.

Our Church

The opportunity for every church in America is enormous. The US population is on its way to being 400 million by 2050, with an aver-age growth of two to three million more people every year.

The world is coming to America and we're not planting churches fast enough to keep up with the population growth. According

---

3   Acts 1:8

to a groundbreaking study of the church in America, 4,000 new churches are started every year in America and in the same time period 3,700 churches close.[4] That's a net gain of only 300 new churches a year for two to three million new people. That's not nearly enough.

To match our population growth, we need to triple our current church-planting efforts every year for the next 30 years, which means your church and my church has incredible growth opportunities. It's not time for church to be an insiders' club for a few people. Now is the time for recapturing our urgency to be the church on a mission, on Jesus' mission, to see new people reached and new churches started in our neighborhoods and cities.

If God wills, that kind of church growth is possible. A historian named Alan Krieder notes that the early church grew by 40 percent per decade for nearly three centuries at a time when Christianity was opposed. Krieder writes: "The early Christians had no mission boards. They did not write treatises about evangelism. After Nero's persecution in the mid-first century, the churches in the Roman Empire closed their worship services to visitors. Deacons stood at the churches' doors, serving as bouncers... and yet the church was growing. Prominent people scorned it. Neighbors discriminated against the Christians in countless petty ways... It was hard to be a Christian... And still the church grew."[5] Scripture tells us

---

4   Pinetops Foundation, 'The Great Opportunity: The American Church in 2050,' 2018, p. 33. The report is available for download at greatopportunity.org (viewed August 13, 2018). I am indebted to the Pinetops Foundation for their research and report.

5   Alan Krieder, 'They Alone Know the Right Way to Live' in Mark Husbands and Jeffrey P. Greenman's Ancient Faith for the Church's Future (Downers Grove, IL; InterVarsity Press, 2008), p. 170.

the church started with 120 people and grew to 3,120 in a single day. Not long after it grew to 10,000.

It happened before. It could happen again. Jesus is still building his church, and this is the greatest time to be alive.

Our Nation

The generation to follow the Millennials is the largest generation in American history. The first wave of Generation Z is now entering college and most of them will be making their decisions about faith over the next 15 years. Reaching Generation Z represents the largest missions opportunity in US history and the clock is ticking.

If we do nothing and the trends we're seeing continue, the result will be that one million youth who were raised in Christian homes in America will leave the Christian faith every year. That means by the year 2050 between 35 and 42 million youth in our generation will no longer affiliate with church or follow Jesus![6] This would be the single largest generational loss of souls in history from those who once called themselves Christians.

We have the opportunity to shift a generation and it begins with the kids who are already in our churches. The impact of just this one thing would reach more people than the first and second Great Awakenings, the African American church growth following the

---

6   'The Great Opportunity: The American Church in 2050', pp. 18–21.

Civil War, the Azusa revivals, and every person who ever came to Christ under Billy Graham's ministry – combined![7]

We can look at America and see a nation losing its moral and spiritual foundations. We can watch the nightly news and feel like darkness is winning. And it would make sense for someone to ask, "What reasons for hope do you have?"

But I don't need multiple reasons, just one: Jesus is alive! We worship a risen Savior who is the Alpha and the Omega, the Beginning and the End, the King of kings and the Lord of lords. Our Jesus has all authority in heaven and on earth and he is with us.

I can choose to look at the darkness and be discouraged or I can lift my eyes to him who sits on heaven's throne and is eager to bless and use his people. The darker it gets, the brighter the light will shine. And Jesus has called us "the light of the world."[8] The light of the world is not what we do; it's who we are as followers of Jesus. Now is the greatest time to let our light shine.

We could wish that God put us in an easier time, in a more comfortable generation, when the culture generally agreed with our values. Or we could see it as a privilege that God Almighty specifically chose for you and me to enter this time in history to light it up in Jesus' name.

---

7   'The Great Opportunity: The American Church in 2050', p. 16.
8   Matthew 5:14

Our World

If you've ever gone to watch a friend run a marathon or compete in a triathlon, then you know the part you don't want to miss is the finish line. That's the most exciting part. It's what you came for.

When we consider the time we're living in, I want you to know that it is very likely we are living in the final lap of the Great Commission race.[9] Never before in history have we been this close to the finish line for fulfilling the mission Jesus gave his followers 2,000 year ago. Never before have we been within reach of the vision of people from every tribe, language, people and nation worshiping Jesus.[10]

There are many indications the Great Commission will be completed in our lifetimes. First, the work of Bible translation is experiencing unprecedented acceleration and collaboration. Just a few years ago there were 1800 languages that still had no Bible translation, but today that number is already less than 1600 and dropping quickly. Bible translation organizations used to complete 15 new translations a year. Now they are doing over a hundred. Organizations and leaders are working together so that all seven billion people on the planet have access to God's word in their heart language by the year 2033.[11] This is happening in our lifetimes.

---

9   The Great Commission is a term given to Jesus' final words in Matthew 28:18-20, which reads, "And Jesus came and said to them, 'All authority in heaven and on earth has been given to me. Go therefore and make disciples of all nations, baptizing them in the name of the Father and of the Son and of the Holy Spirit, teaching them to observe all that I have commanded you. And behold, I am with you always, to the end of the age.'"

10   Revelation 5:9; 7:9–10

11   See illuminations.bible for more information.

But it's about more than having a Bible available. What about people actually reading and engaging with God's word? Now, because of the YouVersion Bible app, we are able to track Bible engagement like never before, as people across the world read Scripture on their devices. And YouVersion is reporting record engagement! Every second of every day an average of 158 people are opening their Bible app to read God's word!

"But what about people who don't read?" you might ask.

It's true that a lot of the people in the world who have never heard of Jesus are a part of oral cultures. They don't read. And yet God is raising up a strong orality movement today, where ministries like the Jesus Film Project are taking the story of Jesus into tribal huts and villages in the most remote places on the planet. They are setting up screens and projectors that show the story of Jesus to the least reached peoples. The Jesus film is the most watched film in history and has been dubbed into nearly 1,700 languages and shown billions of times around the world. Over 500 million people have made decisions to follow Jesus after watching the Jesus Film Project's movies, and they're not done yet.[12]

But what about the deaf?

Currently, there are 70 million deaf people in the world and only two percent of them have received the message of Jesus. The deaf represent the second largest unreached people group on the planet. There are over 350 sign languages globally and not one of them has a full video Bible translation. But this is changing. Projections are

---

12   See jesusfilm.org for more information.

that American Sign Language will have a completed video Bible by 2020 and work is steadily underway across the world to film Bible translations for many more sign languages. The deaf will hear of Jesus in our lifetimes.

Many organizations and individuals across the world are planting churches in those communities where people have still have never heard of Jesus. They are called unreached people groups.

I came across the story of two missionaries who went into a very remote village to see if it was truly unreached. Their first stop was to go the grocer. They asked him, "Can you tell me where I can find Jesus?"

"We don't sell that here," the grocer responded, "But you might want to ask in the market."

So they went to the market and asked again, "Can you tell me where I can find Jesus?"

Again the people said, "Sorry, we don't sell that."

This is the reality for millions and millions of people who are still waiting for the greatest news in the world. They are following the religions of their culture and are caught in a web of fear and lies. They pray and practice religious rituals, but they have no peace, no assurance that God loves them. They have never heard that God sent his Son to save them from their sins and give them eternal life. Unless someone tells them the gospel and they repent, they will suffer the punishment for their sins by being separated from God forever in the greatest possible suffering for the longest possible time – an eternity in hell.[13]

Our Availability

By some mystery of grace, God wants to involve us in his saving work, just like he did with Esther in her time. After the three days of prayer Esther approached the king and "when the king saw Queen Esther standing in the court, she won favor in his sight."[14] Esther stepped outside of her comfort zone and God was there to meet her. God ultimately used her to overthrow the evil plans of Haman and rescue the Jews from death.

Surprisingly, God loves to work through people who, although sinful, still believe in him and step out in faith. The Bible tells us it's through our words that people will hear the word of God.[15] It's through our generosity that God sends out those who preach the saving grace of Jesus.[16] And it's through our prayers that the ends of the earth will be reached.[17]

If you know Jesus, have breath in your lungs and a prayer you can pray, then impact is not only possible, it's mandatory. And the good news is that impact is not about your ability; it's about your

---

13   Matthew 13:40–42, 49–50
14   Esther 5:2
15   Romans 10:14–15; 1 Peter 4:11
16   3 John 5–8; Romans 10:15
17   Matthew 9:36–38

availability. God is looking for people to use and he doesn't look at outward appearances like we do; God looks at the heart.[18]

There is a day coming when we will be in heaven and I like to imagine that when we're there, believers from other generations will lean over the table at the marriage supper of the Lamb and ask us, "What was it like to live in the 21st century when God was doing so much? How was it running the final leg of the race? What did you do with the influence and affluence God gave you?"

I believe you and I have come into God's kingdom for such a time as this! We are living in the greatest time to be alive.

---

18   2 Chronicles 16:9; 1 Samuel 16:7

The Greatest
Time To Be
Alive

TRAINING EXERCISE 7

The Greatest Time To Be Alive

Step 1   As you begin, discuss your experience of Training Exercise 6 (Ask It Exercise). How was this exercise for you? What did you learn? What was difficult? What was God doing in your life?

Step 2   Have one person from your team read Esther chapter 4 aloud.

ESTHER 4 (ESV)

When Mordecai learned all that had been done, Mordecai tore his clothes and put on sackcloth and ashes, and went out into the midst of the city, and he cried out with a loud and bitter cry. He went up to the entrance of the king's gate, for no one was allowed to enter the king's gate clothed in sackcloth. And in every province, wherever the king's command and his decree reached, there was great mourning among the Jews, with fasting and weeping and lamenting, and many of them lay in sackcloth and ashes.

When Esther's young women and her eunuchs came and told her, the queen was deeply distressed. She sent garments to clothe Mordecai, so that he might take off his sackcloth, but he would not accept them. Then Esther called for Hathach, one of the king's eunuchs, who had been appointed to attend her, and ordered him to go to Mordecai to learn what this was and why it was. Hathach went out to Mordecai in the open square of the city in front of the king's gate, and Mordecai told him all that had happened to him, and the exact sum of money that Haman had promised to pay into the king's treasuries for the destruction of the Jews. Mordecai also gave him a copy of the written decree issued in Susa for their destruction, that he might show it to Esther and explain it to her and command her to go to the king to beg his favor and plead with him on behalf of her people. And Hathach went and told Esther what Mordecai had said. Then Esther spoke to Hathach and commanded him to go to Mordecai and say, "All the king's servants and the people of the king's provinces know that if any man or woman goes to the king inside the inner court without being called, there is but one law—to be put to death, except the one to whom the king holds out the golden scepter so that he may live. But as for me, I have not been called to come in to the king these thirty days."

And they told Mordecai what Esther had said. Then Mordecai told them to reply to Esther, "Do not think to yourself that in the king's palace you will escape any more than all the other Jews. For if you keep silent at this time, relief and deliverance will rise for the Jews from another place, but you and your father's house will perish. And who knows whether you have not come to the kingdom for such a time as this?" Then Esther told them to reply to Mordecai, "Go, gather all the Jews to be found in Susa, and hold a fast on my behalf, and do not eat or drink for three days, night or day. I and my young women will also fast as you do. Then I will go to the king, though it is against the law, and if I perish, I perish." Mordecai then went away and did everything as Esther had ordered him.

Step 3   What do you notice from this story? Which phrase or sentence most stands out to you? Write it down, then share these among your team.

_____

_____

_____

Step 4   The rest of this exercise is a chance for you and your team to celebrate the completion of *Giving Together*, while also pushing outside of your comfort zone. Your assignment is to go to an ethnic restaurant with your team for dinner. Choose something different, something out of your comfort zone. You may want to begin by asking: What nationalities of people are around us? Who has God drawn to our city? And then decide as a team which country's food you want to try.

Step 5   Next you'll need to choose a date and time that works for a majority of your team.

_____

_____

_____

Step 6   You'll need four volunteers for the following roles:

1)   One person should choose a restaurant from whatever ethnic genre your team decided and make a reservation if you can. If there is a foodie on your team, this would be a great role for that person.

2)   Another person can research the demographics, politics and economics of that country. The CIA World Factbook website is a good place to start. The idea here is to get a big picture overview of the country to bring your team up to speed. This would be a good role for a visionary or the entrepreneur in your group – someone who likes to see the big picture.

3)   A third person can look up current events in that country. If you have a person on your team who loves politics and the news and current events, this would be a great job for them.

4)   A fourth person can learn about the spiritual condition and prayer needs of that nation. One great place to start would be to order a copy of the book *Operation World* by Jason Mandryk. If someone on your team loves to travel and see the world, they would be a good fit for this role.

Step 7   Each of these volunteers should bring a five-minute summary of their research to share when you meet at the restaurant.

Step 8   Pray for God to open doors for relationships with people who you'll meet at the restaurant.

Step 9   Over dinner have each of the people who did research share their five-minute summaries of what they learned and what stood out to them.

Step 10   Initiate conversation with your server about the needs of their native country. Remember, success doesn't equal the perfect plan or a dramatic story to tell. Success is risking in the right direction for the right reason.

Step 11   Pray together for the nation you chose and the people you met. Remember that Esther's big mission began with prayer. And even more, Jesus commanded prayer to be our first step in his mission as well when he said, "The harvest is plentiful, but the laborers are few; therefore pray earnestly to the Lord of the harvest to send out laborers into his harvest."[19]

---

19   Matthew 9:37–38

Step 12   Tip generously.

Step 13   <u>Journal:</u> How did God lead you? What happened? What did you learn? What did God stir in your heart? Are there any next steps you sense God leading you to take? Discuss these with each other.

_____

_____

_____

_____

_____

_____

_____

_____

THIS WEEK'S VIDEO:

givingtogether.video/impact

Summiting

A friend of mine recently celebrated his son's high school graduation with a trip to Tanzania to climb Africa's tallest mountain, Mount Kilimanjaro. After they completed it, I received a text message with a picture of him on the icy pinnacle at 19,341 feet. His message read:

"Summited about 7am on 7/2 and then down all the way yesterday about 1pm... Craziest/hardest thing I've ever done... Crazy ice and winds."

Summiting is never easy. There are many chances to give up and turn back. But Todd and Zach kept going amidst the resistance and they made it to the top. This is what I want for you with giving. God is on a mission to transform you into the image Jesus. This is your destiny.[1] This is not simply for some Christians; this is God's plan for all Christians. And a major part of the transformation is becoming a person like him, who has a heartbeat of generosity. This is what it means to summit.

Summiting is not an amount. It's not a percentage you give. It means developing a heartbeat of generosity. I realize that might sound like one of the craziest and hardest things you've ever done. Surely there will be many obstacles, many times you and I take our eyes off of Jesus and, like Peter, begin to sink. But we are promised that he who began a good work in us will bring it to completion.[2] Scripture says, "Just as we have borne the image of the man of dust, we shall also bear the image of the man of heaven."[3] This is our future.

You have come a long way in this adventure. You have kept climbing amidst crazy ice and winds. It's not been easy. You could have given up and turned back, but you didn't. So keep climbing, brothers and sisters! God is calling you up, and you will surely summit.

---

1   Romans 8:29
2   Philippians 1:6
3   1 Corinthians 15:49

To share your
Giving Together story with us,
write to us at
stories@gospelpatrons.org

For more copies of **Giving Together**,
visit us at gospelpatrons.org

About the Artist

JOHN-MARK WARKENTIN built his career at an ad agency, before transitioning to work as the Chief Innovator for Gospel Patrons. He is the creator of gospelpatrons.org, the director of six short films, and the designer of *Gospel Patrons* and *Giving Together*.

John-Mark lives in Orange County, California with his wife and four children. To see more of his work or to contact John-Mark, visit: gospelpatrons.org

About the Author

JOHN RINEHART is an author, speaker, and the founder of Gospel Patrons. His first book *Gospel Patrons* tells three stories from history about business leaders who were behind the scenes fueling amazing movements of God. He speaks widely at conferences and churches.

John has a business degree from Biola University and a Masters of Divinity from Talbot School of Theology. He lives in Orange County, California with his wife and two children. To learn more or to contact John, visit: gospelpatrons.org

Acknowledgments

Thank you for reading this book!

I hope it felt like a fun gift to receive and helped you make new connections with God and other people. It was not an easy book to write, but took three years to develop because the ideas and insights were drawn from so many relationships and conversations.

Thank you to Jesus! Thank you for freeing us from "the cares of the world and the deceitfulness of riches and the desires for other things" so that we can be people who hear the word and bear fruit, thirty, sixty and a hundredfold.

Thank you to my wife Renée. Your sense of adventure got this whole thing started and it's been the greatest ride of our lives. Thank you for teaching me so much about God's heart by how you live day in and day out. I love you!

Thank you to John-Mark Warkentin. Wow! The journey just keeps getting better and better. Thank you for being my friend and partner in the gospel. Working with you is one of God's greatest gifts to me.

Thank you to Caleb and Laura. You make all the difference. There are not enough words to say thank you.

Thank you to Brian Petersen. You change the game for us. Thank you for being a great friend and a joy to work with.

Thank you to Simon and Bex. We talked about the concept of this book at your home during an unforgettable season for our family. Thanks for blessing us with your rich friendship and true partnership.

Thank you to Josh Wilson. You enable so much good to happen. Thank you for assisting me in a hundred different ways. I believe in you.

Thank you to Ron and Pam. Your lives make generosity look so attractive and inspire me to get this message out to the world. Thank you for believing in this book and hosting the first beta group.

Thank you to Kevin and Leslie and Rob and Amber. The stories from your beta group convinced me that this experience could be life-giving to thousands more people. Thank you for following Jesus and joining us on this thrilling adventure.

Thank you to Mart and Diana. Your strong belief in us is humbling and it was you who spoke the line that became the title of this book: "Our family has no greater joy then when we're giving together." May this book spread that joy to many more families.

Thank you to Todd and Susan. You have taught me so much by your lives and opened up so many doors for me. Thank you for your example of leading a world-changing movement. I hope to follow in your steps.

Thank you to Akeel and Joy. Your passion for the gospel and Gospel Patrons have deeply blessed me. Thank you for partnering with us in so many significant ways. The best is yet to come.

Thank you to Dan and Evelyn. You raised an adventurous and generous daughter who has been God's gift to me. We plan to keep that legacy going. Thank you for everything.

Thank you to Catherine Muthey. There is no telling how far we've flown on your faithful prayers. Thank you for joining us on the journey.

Thank you to Kirsten McKinlay and Tammy Ditmore for your insightful editing and passion for commas, footnotes, and truth. This is a better book because of you.

Thank you to Janice Worth. Your story and friendship have deeply impacted me and I pray this book will carry your example to many more who need to climb Everest.

Thank you to Jim and Kristin. You have a massive sense of adventure and a great heart for God. Thanks for believing in me and GP amidst some cloudy weather. I look forward to the bright adventures we'll have together in the years ahead.

Thank you to Rod and Pam. Only heaven will reveal the global and eternal impact of your lives. If this book inspires one family to live like you, it will be worth it. Thank you for your friendship.

Thank you to Aaron and Michelle. I'll never forget how God wove our paths together. Thank you for saying "Yes" in that moment and several others. I can't wait to partner with you more.

Thank you to Tim and Steph. Your encouragement and partnership has been wind in our sails. Thank you for believing and living this message.

Thank you to Mark Speeter. You have been a great friend and pastor to me these last two years. Thank you for being a man full of faith and of the Holy Spirit.

Thank you to Steve and Chere Rinehart. What can I say? You gave me life. You gave me my name. You gave me love. You gave me an education. You fed me for eighteen years... and I ate a lot! You took risks and made sacrifices to give me opportunities in life you never had. You followed Jesus. You loved the Bible. You sang God's praises. You taught me how to live. You gave your lives for mine, day in and day out. Thank you is not enough. I love you both.

Lastly, to my kids, Willow and Malachi. You both give me so much joy. Let's keep learning to live with a heartbeat of generosity until the day Jesus calls us home.

Behind every great movement
of God, there are those
who go first in giving.

 GOSPEL
PATRONS.ORG

Gospel Patrons

People Whose Generosity Changed The World

John Rinehart

MORE

THAN

A PRO

TODD PETERSON · SUSAN PETERSON
ROY PETERSON · LOUIE GIGLIO

GOSPEL
PATRONS.ORG

Every Village in India

ED FOSTER · DAS

GOSPEL PATRONS.ORG

Gospel Patrons is a non-profit organization whose mission is to inspire and empower a generation of Gospel Patrons. We do this in five ways:

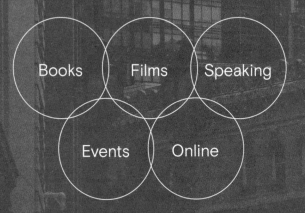

Books   Films   Speaking

Events   Online

Our vision is to fuel great movements of God around the world by helping many more men and women to passionately play their part in God's kingdom. You can learn more and find free articles, films, and videos at **gospelpatrons.org**

GOSPEL
PATRONS.ORG